"Practice What You Preach!"

Godly Prophetic Poetry

Fiya
(Christopher Barrett)

This book of verse is dedicated to my Princes and Princesses:

Akua, Keziah, Isaiah, Malachi, Shanaya, Kyra & Caiden-Jahmai "CJ"

(Fiya), Christopher Barrett
Author

Contents

Bonus:

Preface

Our time and experience inspires us to appreciate the simple things in life. One can only grasp the spiritual gift that gives utterance to our conscious, to generously submit to something not seen. Sacrifice is a critical choice but charitable in serving others. This Godly character is not limited to earthly invitations, instead it's a dedication to God's love.

Christopher Barrett presents God's free gift of love in a language that ignites the spirit. In this collection of poems, Christopher extends his experience to readers as an act of faith. Each stanza are pillars of fire with over forty years of complete submission to the Creator. Christopher has prepared a way for godly poetry as a sign of sacrifice.

Andrew M. Foster

Author, Publisher, Pioneer

Fire

It's your choice!
I have given you an ultimatum
it's up to you now to choose the way,
the right road which will lead you closer to me

I have respect for you as a disciple of my gospel.
Only a character such as yours
can be used in such a way
that I and only I receive all the glory,
in an extremely unique way

Your life is in my hands now,
do not allow others to deter you
or obstruct you in the ministry,
to which I have called you to
live, preach & teach

Yes, you are precious in my spirit
& no one can take that away say I,
what I have blessed no man can curse

Thank you. For obeying my voice
it's not always easy I know,
it's by my spirit & nothing else you can try
will bring the same result

I love you & when you are alone,
I especially love you,
because you & I are in communion,
& I look forward to listening to you,
to bless you, my son

Don't ever change,
you are perfect in my sight
& that is what matters most,
that I am pleased

Blessings will fall on you just wait & see!!!

By inspiration of the Holy Spirit: 17/02/99

Credit: Doreen Mclaughlin, 170299

Humanity Seeks That Peace Of Mind!

I thought at one point, that I had that peace of mind.
Peace of mind I say that humanity seeks for.

But then if humanity is seeking for that peace of mind,
don't you think that everybody should know their own
state of mind.

Well it seems that humanity has declared already
they're at peace, providing that the next person
doesn't take a liberty.
But guess what?

That peace of mind that the human race is searching
for, like they are entering some kind of rat race starts
from within our state of mind.

Sympathy at one point is what humanity craves for
but the spirit, the inner person wants is that peace of
mind.

So what you gonna do?

Are you gonna go around blaming everybody else for
your existence or you gonna quit?

So the best thing for me to do, instead of blaming someone or something, be at peace from within myself first, then my mind will be at peace.

Finally these words came to mind, you are what you think of yourself.

Have a positive mental thinking attitude, towards your seeking that peace of mind.

Give it up!

What are you holding on to!

Give it up!

If that which you are holding on too, is too hard to let go, then you've got to ask yourself is it good or bad for me!

After asking this question to yourself
are you gonna, give it up or hold on!

You see when you say this statement over and over again you think to yourself, what do I give up!

Whatever you're going to give up!

GIVE IT UP WITH A PURE HEART!

FIRE!

*Prince's Trust 10/01/98

Where are you going?

JESUS IS THE WAY!

Do you know I ask myself this question all the time!

Where are you going?

If you know, are you going to tell someone else? Or you're gonna go where you're going!

The reason why I ask this question is because people of society, thinks that they know where their going!

But hey!

I've got news for you "Boast not thyself of tomorrow; for thou knowest not what a day may bring forth."

Book of Proverbs Chapter 27 vs 1

Prince's Trust 09/30/98

Where are you?

I look here, there, everywhere

where are you?

You said, you'll always be there for me
but next minute you're here, and then you're gone

Where are you?

I begin to lose hope and trust in you, because you say
one thing, and you mean another thing

Where are you?

I start to worry, but then hey I know where you are!

You're right here, within me!

Camp America: 06/23/98

Please come!

Time and time again, I ask you

Please come!

When you are near or far,
I plead you to come

Please! Come home to me?

I need to know you are here within me

Camp America: 08/05/98

I do need you!

Hey!

I do need you, and I'm not scared to show it to.

So when I say I need you, please don't go on like you don't need me too.

Because life's pattern says we all need each other too.

Camp America: 06/24/98

Sorry!

Sorry for hurting you!
Sorry I keep on saying that word
I really do mean what I say,

Sorry!

When I say this word, please find somewhere in your
heart to forgive me, when I keep on repeating and
continuing to hurt you, I know that this is not me!

What I'm trying to say in a short way, is I must learn
to forgive myself, before I can start to
forgive others!

Sorry!

Give strength!

When I'm weak, I look to get strength
When I'm down, I ask to be lifted up

One thing I've learnt, is when you give strength
to others, it comes back to you

Give the strength you have inside your heart
because they say

What goes around comes around

So positive breeds positive and negative
produces negative

So how can you get strengthened by a negative
spirit?

By giving the strength we have in our hearts, to
those who are weak in spirit!

GIVE STRENGTH!

Camp America: 7/03/98

God loves you believe me!

Believe me, when I say I love you!
Believe in me please because there's no one else, I can
say this too!

When I say these words, I mean what I say!

Believe me!

If you don't believe me, who will?
I ask this time and time again!

Believe me!

You said you would be there for me when I needed
somebody; well believe me the time is now!

Everybody tells me, believe in yourself first believe
me; I know what they are saying right now!

But everybody sometimes, in their lives needs
somebody or some to believe in them!

Believe me I know that we've all been down this path!

So if someone asks you to believe in them and
everybody tells me believe in yourself first, then
believe in me please show them the way, how to

believe in themselves!

I know how this feels,

BELIEVE ME!

Camp America: 08/05/98

I love you 🖤

Oh Lord do I love you!

You loved me first, by sending your only begotten son on Calvary, where he died on the cross for you and me!

You said Lord; your love covers all multitudes of sins!

O Lord do I love you!

Lord I love you because in you there's no sin or unrighteousness!

My love for you, first came out of you!

O Lord do I love you!

Ruach Ministries 18/12/98

Let's love

Let's love because love breaks through all things!

Let's love in spirit and truth, not physical lust!

All love; love's everybody, everything and everyone despite of colour or creed!

Let's love cause when you learn to love from within, you will have unconditional love!

Camp America: 22/06/98

Joy!

Joy is in the heart, why is that we can't find this Joy?

Where are you, I'm looking for you!

Joy, you mean so much to me!

When I'm upset I think of your beautiful name!

Joy!

Camp America: 06/09/98

Let your love flow!

Let your love flow within me, so I can be whole again
Feeling like this without the flow of your love, makes
me feel empty inside

Let your love flow through me because without you,
there is no me!
They say that you never forget your first love!
Well that is true, yeah true love which I yearn for the
flow, day in and day out

Please, let your love flow so others can see the true
beauty of your love
We look here, there and everywhere but not within, so
let your love flow within me
They say love is blind, too blind to see!

Well they say that but I know when your love flows
out of me, it's like a bright light you see.
So maybe their love is an everlasting love within you
and me.

When you have the true flowing of love in your life, it
makes you feel on top of the world.
On top of the world, so that you see!
What are you seeing? Don't forget what they say about
love!

Is it their love? My love, whose love is it?
One thing I know, when you let your love flow I can
see what you see
Because true love, loves everybody and respects
everybody

Thinking on his goodness!

When I think on his goodness, I just want to cry.
Cry you ask me why?

Because on his goodness I can lift up my
hands and praise him.
You say what do I have to praise him for?
Praise him because I have arms, legs, eyes to see, ears
to hear and my whole body is in good function. That
is why I think on his goodness!

Thinking on his goodness, makes me understand that
I woke up by his grace.
Grace you asking me in such a confused state!
This is why you're abused, confused but not total out
of use!

The Word of God states "For the ways of man are
before the eyes of the Lord, and he pondereth all his
goings."
Book of Proverbs Chapter 5 vs 21

So while I'm thinking on his goodness he's thinking in
deep thought about all my goings!

Ruach Ministries 12/12/98

The price is free!

The price is free, because God said it is for you & for me!

The price is free, because our Lord & Saviour has come to set us all free!

For the law of the spirit of life in Christ Jesus has, made me free from the law of sin and death.

For what the law could not do in that it was weak through the FLESH, God did by sending his own son in the likeness of sin.

He condemned sin in the flesh that the righteous requirement of the law might be fulfilled in who do not walk according to the FLESH but according to the spirit.

ROMANS 8: 2-4

So do we have a choice to receive this free gift, without paying the old rugged cross!

Those who are in the FLESH cannot PLEASE God.

ROMANS 8: 8

For he who sows to his FLESH will of the FLESH reap corruption, but he who sows to the SPIRIT will of the SPIRIT reap everlasting life.

GALATIANS 6: 8

But now having been set free from sin, & having become slaves of God, you have your fruit to holiness, & the end everlasting life.

For the WAGES of sin is DEATH, but the GIFT of God is
eternal life in Christ Jesus our Lord.

ROMANS 6: 22-23

So what price are you willing to pay?

Is it by the FLESH or by SPIRIT?

Behold, I am with you and will keep you wherever you go, and will bring you back to this land. For I will not leave you until I have done that what I have spoken to you.

GENESIS 28: 15

So what you gonna do?

I'll leave it up to you!

But don't forget
the price is free!

Ruach Ministers 27/01/99

The breath of fresh air!

This fresh air that we all share, whose is it?
Is it black air or white air?

The breath of fresh air!

The fact remains it is the law of God's breath of
fresh air!

So you're asking me now about the law of God!

You're think what's that gotta do with the freshness
of the air?

Well the law of gravity says what goes up must come
down!

GOD loved us all, so let's live in peace and share this
breath of fresh air!

Z-bar 01/02/99

Believe Jesus!

JESUS CHRIST

Do you believe Jesus?

Maybe your answer is yes or no, but one thing I know
he believes in us.

And the Lord said unto Moses, How long will this
people provoke me? And how long will it be ere they
believe me, for all the signs which I have shewed
among them?

Book of Numbers Chapter 14 vs 11

Do you believe Jesus?

Jesus says 'Believe ye that I am able to do this?'

Book of St. Matthew Chapter 9 vs 28

Do you believe Jesus?
What's your answer now, is it yes or no?

Do you need more signs in your life to believe Jesus!

In the beginning was the Word, and the Word was with GOD, and the Word was GOD.

The same was in the beginning with GOD.
All things were made by him and without him was anything made.

Book of St. John 1 vs 1-3

Do you believe Jesus?

He hath made everything beautiful in his time; also he hath set the world in their heart, so that no man can find out the work that God maketh for the beginning to the end

Book of Ecclesiastes Chapter 3 vs 11

Do you believe Jesus?

Not everybody is going to believe Jesus but 'The simple believeth every word but the prudent man looketh well to his going

Book of Proverbs Chapter 14 vs 15

You see Jesus wants us to believe in him because he said 'That they all may be one as thou father, art in me and I in thee, that they also may be one in us: that world may believe that thou hast sent me

Believing in something which you can't see can
be frightening
But without faith it is impossible to please him: for he
that cometh to God must believe that He is, and that
He is a rewarder of them that diligently
seek him

Book of Hebrews Chapter 11 vs 6

So believing in Jesus I must have faith in him.

Do you believe Jesus now?

Ruach Ministries 03/01/99

I was born to be free!

Free I was Born to be from the beginning of these words is me

Through the creature becomes you and me that is why these words are within thee.

Not knowing that in the beginning was he that made us free, though his words now and forever more. I was born to be free.

In these words is he for without these words nothing would be.

So now you have taken the time to read these words, I hope you begin to be free.

You see if you don't believe that you were born to be free, no one else but He that can make you see.

That you were born to be free.

With the same desires which everybody wants is to be free

But there's one thing I would like the world to know, is that I was born to be free.

Free for everybody else to see, just like you and me, I know that we were all born to be free.

Finishing off with a few words we all say and hope we believe in, is that you are what you eat,

I'm eating freedom!

A long path to freedom

The spirit indeed is willing but the flesh is weak!

Matthew 26 vs 41,

From, the beginning of creation the creator has built a world, built with different paths to freedom

But each spirit has their own path to freedom

Yeah!

They say everyone or everybody is responsible for their own actions, meaning from a certain age we have been taught how to live and how to survive

But we tend to forget that the body our spirit rest in is here only for a time

Time waits for nobody not for you or me; it has simply been given to us for free

So now you can see your own long path to freedom because only you and the creator can overcome your negative situations

You see, we are used to depending on our own intellect or we gather knowledge to direct the body and mind to a so call point of freedom

But one thing is for sure, that is the spirit of the creator is an all seeing all knowing presence

No matter what we choose to do with our bodies and minds, we cannot escape the divine order of the path of freedom

So let's all learn to Trust in the Lord with all thine heart, and learn not onto thine own understanding. In all thy ways acknowledge him, and he shall direct thy paths.

Proverbs 3 vs 5-6

Let me go!

Let me go, because I want to be free!
Let me go, it's not between you and me!

Why do you want to hold back?

Just let me go!

All I ask of you is to set me free!
When I'm free of mental slavery,
Then my spirit can go where it pleases!

So please set me free,
So I can be me!

Camp America: 06/24/98

SPIRIT!

Spirit set me free, which spirits are these!

Black spirit, white spirit, female spirit and
male spirit, which spirits of the Creator are within
thee!

You see at the end of the day, you can't
see the spirit that has come too set you free!

So when you have found the true spirit,
that has come to set us all free!

TELL SOMEBODY!

Camp America: 22/06/98

Why me?

Why me?
I don't know why it's between you and me!

I ask myself this question all the time!
Why me?

When you don't have an answer be strong,
look within yourself!

I know me, because there's no one like me,
that's why it's me!

Jesus loves us all, he told me so!

Camp America: 22/06/98

Why they trouble me!

Why they trouble me,
I don't Know
I ask myself this question all the time!

Why they trouble me?

Is it because of my colour
or
The spirit that reigns within me!

Maybe they don't like what they see!
I really don't know why they don't like me!

One thing I know for sure,
Is that not everybody is going to like me!

Why they trouble me?

ONLY GOD KNOWS!

Don't strike!

Don't strike, because you leave pain & sorrow!
Don't strike, because it shows who's strong & who's
weak!
The strong are those taking the beating!
And the weak, are those who give in

WHY!

You ask in dismay!

Well, strong is the person who can forgive that person
inflicting pain upon them, then moves on in life!

Weak is the person just sticking out their anger and
frustrations upon the person!

They say sticks and stones may break my bones but
words will never hurt me!

THAT'S A LIE!

Don't strike whether it, be PHYSICAL or VERBAL
It leaves the person with pain
ETERNAL!

This poem is dedicated to those who have gone through Domestic Violence!

College work 16/12/98

Camp America: 06/10/98

Empire Windrush!

I was a child with my own people!
I was a child with my own state of mind!

I remember the cock crowing early in the morning,
waking me up for my morning chores!
It was so sweet hearing that beautiful sound and the
cool breeze, blowing against my lovely brown skin
seeing the big red sun such afar!

Then I see my family and friends packing their things
together! I think to myself what is going on, are we
going on a trip or seeing other family members in
town!

Then I hear voices above me all around me shouting
out "The Windrush is coming the Windrush is
coming. Quick, quick get all your belongings
together".

Then before I could blink I'm scared and cold in
another country, on this large boat floating away from
my beautiful surroundings!

They called this a trip on the Empire Windrush!

Lambeth College: 28/01/99

Bonus

COLOUR!

Roses are Red, Violets are Blue
I AM made just as beautiful like you

No matter what the COLOUR of your skin is just
remember that I AM the Creator, who created and
made you

Remember it is said, that beauty is in the eyes of the
beholder. So what are you seeing or holding if you are
naturally being the beautiful COLOUR which you are
created to be

Remember inner beauty is one of many great gifts
given to the beholder, if they sincerely want to shine
their AUTHENTIC designed COLOUR which you
are created to do in reflection of your uniqueness that
everybody processes from BIRTH

NEVER, NEVER, NEVER allow anyone or thing
from this world or the supernatural world who doesn't
appreciate you being AUTHENTIC and shining
through your inner beauty, the COLOUR which you

are created to be unique and not being
ARTIFICIALLY INTELLIGENT or SYNTHETIC
that's made not created but made by human hands
Selah

COLOUR is just a visual uniqueness of beauty and
being AUTHENTIC from your inner being, which is
BE WHO YOU BE and that's what you will discover
for yourselves what purpose is for you to fulfil your
DESTINY

For I know the thoughts that I think toward you, says
the LORD, thoughts of shalom, and not of evil, to
give you hope in your latter end
Jeremiah 29 vs 11

Before I formed you in the belly I knew you, and
before you came forth out of the womb I sanctified
you; I have appointed you a prophet to the nations
Jeremiah 1 vs 5

My Butterfly!

My first sight of this unique Butterfly, I'd became irritated and scared

Yes scared you're probably wondering and thinking to yourself, how can you be so scared of such beauty and uniqueness?

Well, My Butterfly showed ME (Mental Evaluation) a very important thing about LIFE and CHANGE

Changes are inevitable in life and the most beneficial and beautifulest thing that My Butterfly taught ME (Motivational Experiences) is to embrace the changes in our lives and to go through the metamorphosis processing stages completely

This is essential and critical for our God given born purpose to fulfil because you will either end up doing two things in your decision making

Either complain inwardly, thinking that God can't hear your thoughts and heart - "Would God find this out? For He knows the secrets of the heart."
Psalm 44 vs 21

Or embrace the inevitable changes and rejoice in the momentum movement of the Holy Spirit showing you your destiny to be established for His ultimate plan for your life. "Commit to the LORD whatever you do, and he will establish your plans."
Proverbs 16 vs 3

My Butterfly I AM so grateful for your lessons of changes in life...
Selah

THE END

Printed in Great Britain
by Amazon

40265501R00036